Learning English with the Bible

ANSWER GUIDE

BY LOUISE M. EBNER

AMG

PUBLISHERS

6815 Shallowford Road
Chattanooga, TN 37421

ISBN 0-89957-604-4

Printed in the United States of America
01 00   9 8 7

Answer Guide for
Learning English with the Bible

A SYSTEMATIC APPROACH TO BIBLE-BASED ENGLISH GRAMMAR

BY
LOUISE M. EBNER

JOHN 20:31

"BUT THESE ARE WRITTEN, THAT YE MIGHT BELIEVE THAT
JESUS IS THE CHRIST, THE SON OF GOD; AND THAT BELIEVING
YE MIGHT HAVE LIFE THROUGH HIS NAME."

TABLE OF CONTENTS

PART I
LEARNING PARTS OF SPEECH

PART II
USING PARTS OF SPEECH

PART III
VERBALS

PART IV
SENTENCE STRUCTURE

SUGGESTIONS FOR COMPOSITION

Exercises entitled **"EXPLORING TRUTHS"** are found at the end of chapters.

ANSWER BOOKLET

Chapter 1

1. Jesus, Bethlehem, Judaea, days, Herod, king, men, east, Jeruslaem, King, Jews.

2. star, east

3. Herod, King, things, Jerusalem

4. priests, scribes, people, Christ

5. Bethlehem, Judaea, prophet, Bethlehem, land, Judaea, least, princes, Judah, Governor, people, Israel

EXERCISE 2

A noun is the name of a person, place, thing, idea or quality.

EXERCISES 3, 4, 5, 6

Answers will vary.

EXERCISE 7

	(PR)	(CM)	(CM-AB)	(CM-CN)
1.	Herod,	men,	time,	star

	(PR)	(CM)	(CM, CN)
2.	Bethlehem,	child,	word.

	(CM)	(CM-CN)	(CM)	(CM)
3.	king,	star,	east,	child

	(CN-CL)	(CM)	(CM-CN)	(CM-AB)
4.	group,	men,	star,	joy

EXERCISES 8 and 9

Answers will vary.

TEST ON NOUNS

Line 1 – proverbs, Solomon, son, David, king, Israel

Line 2 – wisdom, instruction, words, understanding

Line 3 – instruction, wisdom, justice, judgment, equity

Lines 4, 5 – subtility, simple, man, knowledge, discretion

Lines 6, 7 – man, learning, man, understanding, counsels

Lines 8, 9 – proverb, interpretation, words, wise, sayings

Lines 10, 11 – fear, Lord, beginning, knowledge, fools, wisdom, instruction

Lines 12, 13 – son, instruction, father, law, mother

Chapter 2

EXERCISE 1

A pronoun is a word used as a substitute for a noun.

EXERCISE 3

I	we
you	you
he, she, it	they

EXERCISE 4

my, mine	our, ours
your, yours	your, yours
his, her, hers, its	their, theirs

EXERCISE 5

me	us
you	you
him, her, it	them

EXERCISE 6

1. I
2. their, theirs
3. we
4. he
5. them
6. you
7. our, ours
8. your, yours
9. her
10. my, mine

EXERCISE 7

masculine, feminine, neuter

EXERCISE 8

1. they, they, his, him
2. they, their, they, him
3. they, they, their
4. they, his, I, you
5. him
6. he, he, his
7. they, it, I, my

EXERCISE 9

1. few
2. all
3. any
4. all, none, one
5. nothing
6. some, some
7. all, all, none
8. many
9. many
10. nothing, neither

EXERCISE 10

1. This
2. (*These* is a demonstrative adjective.)
3. these
4. that
5. such
6. that
7. these
8. such
9. that

EXERCISE 11

this, that, these, those, such

EXERCISE 12

who, whose, whom, which, what

EXERCISE 13

1. Who
2. whom
3. What
4. whom, whom
5. Who
6. Which
7. Which
8. Whose

EXERCISE 14

myself	ourselves
yourself	yourselves
himself, herself, itself	themselves

EXERCISE 15

1. themselves
2. yourselves
3. himself
4. yourselves
5. myself
6. himself
7. ourselves

EXERCISE 16

who, whose, whom, which, that

TEST ON PRONOUNS

1. he (personal), that (relative), he (personal), all (indefinite), that (relative), all (indefinite), which (relative), he (personal)
2. that (demonstrative), which (relative)
3. her (personal), they (personal)
4. none
5. his (personal), they (personal), which (relative)
6. he (personal), his (personal)
7. he (personal), that (relative), his (personal), he (personal), he (personal)
8. he (personal), that (relative), it (personal), which (relative), he (personal)

3

EXERCISE 1

A verb is a word that expresses action or shows a condition or state.

EXERCISE 2

1. preached	6. went
2. wrote	7. baptized, confessed
3. prepared	8. came
4. wore, had	9. warned
5. ate	10. baptized, comes, will baptize

EXERCISE 3

Answers will vary. Accept any verbs listed under Lesson 3-C.

EXERCISE 4

Answers will vary.

1. is
2. was
3. should be, are
4. is, are
5. become

EXERCISE 5

1. felt – l.v., heard – a.v.
2. spoke – a.v., became – l.v.
3. built – a.v.
4. was – l.v.
5. sounded – a.v.
6. sounded – l.v.
7. looked – a.v.
8. looked – a.v.
9. removed – a.v., looked – a.v.
10. looked – l.v., ended – a.v.

EXERCISE 6

1. came – a.v.
2. was baptized – a.v., went – a.v., were opened – a.v., saw – a.v.
3. said – a.v., is – l.v., am – l.v.
4. was led – a.v., was tempted – a.v.
5. fasted – a.v., was – l.v.

6. came – a.v., said – a.v., are – l.v., command – a.v.
7. replied – a.v., shall live – a.v., proceeds – a.v.
8. tempted – a.v.
9. said – a.v., is written – a.v., shall worship – a.v., shall serve – a.v.
10. left – a.v., ministered – a.v.

EXERCISE 7

1. created – tr.
2. was – intr.
3. was – intr.
4. moved – intr.
5. said – tr., let be – intr., was – intr.
6. was – intr., saw – tr.
7. divided – tr.
8. called – tr.
9. called – tr.
10. were – intr.

TEST ON VERBS

1. Answers will vary. See Lesson 3-C.
2. Answers will vary. See Lesson 3-D.
3. a. is – intr., is – intr.
   b. comes – intr., comes – intr., is – intr.
   c. shall guide – tr., shall destroy – tr.
   d. profit – intr., delivereth – intr.
   e. is – intr., winneth – tr., is – intr.

Chapter 4

EXERCISE 1

1. beautiful
2. great, greater, lesser (two – limiting adjective)
3. moving, open
4. large, living, winged (every – limiting adjective)
5. wild (all – limiting adjective)
6. own
7. whole
8. (seventh, all – limiting adjectives)
9. pleasant, good
10. good, alone, help

NOTE: The articles, possessive pronouns, and indefinite pronouns are not descriptive adjectives.

EXERCISE 2

1. a   2. an   3. the

EXERCISE 3

1. this   3. these   5. such
2. that   4. those

EXERCISE 4

1. What (P)
2. what
3. who (P)
4. The
5. That, contrary, Biblical
6. Those, pleasing
7. all, profitable
8. all (P), the
9. the, any (P), that (P), that (P)
10. Everyone (P), them (P), they (P), filthy, none (P), good, one (P)

TEST ON ADJECTIVES

1. Isaiah's, the, a
2. the, the, six
3. Holy, holy, holy, the, the whole, full
4. a, unclean
5. One, a live, Isaiah's
6. the
7. These, true, the
8. all

Chapter 5

EXERCISE 1

1. not
2. Henceforth, to, fro, about
3. up
4. fitly, together
5. fast
6. patiently
7. freely
8. boldly

EXERCISE 2

1. once
2. again
3. quickly
4. soon
5. never, not
6. quite
7. willfully
8. yesterday, today, forever
9. also
10. fully

EXERCISE 3

Answers will vary – accordingly, also, besides, consequently, furthermore, hence, however, indeed, likewise, moreover, nevertheless, still, then, thus, therefore.

EXERCISE 4

1. how   2. when   3. where   4. why

EXERCISE 5

1. When   2. Where   3. why

TEST ON ADVERBS

1. a. how?
   b. when?
   c. where?
   d. to what extent?
   e. how much?

2. a. verb
   b. adverb
   c. adjective

3. adverbial nouns

4. a. sparingly, also, sparingly, bountifully, also, bountifully
   b. Today, not
   c. How, so
   d. Then, away
   e. Evening, morning, aloud
   f. up, early
   g. only, not
   h. godly
   i. then, not
   j. fast, not, again

Chapter 6

EXERCISE 1

1. of God, upon the face, of the waters
2. from the darkness
3. in the midst, of the waters, from the waters
4. under the firmament, from the waters, above the firmament
5. of the waters
6. after his own kind, in itself, upon the earth
7. in the Father, in me
8. unto you, of myself, in me
9. for the very work's sake
10. unto you, on me, unto my Father

TEST ON PREPOSITIONS

I. Answers will vary. See page 47.

II. preposition, noun, pronoun, adjective

III. a. for good
        to them
        to them
        according to His purpose
    b. to them
        of God
        to them
        on his name
    c. in any other
        under heaven
        among men
    d. in perfect peace
        on thee
        in thee
    e. at the door
        to him
        with him
        with me

Chapter 7

EXERCISE 1

    1. and
    2. but
    3. or
    4. nor
    5. for
    6. so
    7. yet

EXERCISE 2

    1. and
    2. but
    3. or
    4. for, and
    5. and
    6. nor
    7. and

EXERCISE 3
    1. either . . . or
    2. neither . . . nor
    3. not only . . . but also
    4. both . . . and

EXERCISE 4
    1. not only . . . but also
    2. both . . . and
    3. not only . . . but also

TEST ON CONJUNCTIVES

    1. for
    2. and
    3. yet
    4. and
    5. but, and
    6. both, and, but
    7. and, for

Chapter 8

EXERCISE 1
1. behold
2. Alas
3. oh
4. Hurrah

EXERCISE 2
Answers will vary. See Lesson 8-B.

EXERCISE 3
1. therefore
2. indeed
3. And I intreat thee also
4. And this I say
5. Likewise

Test on Interjections

1. Behold
2. Oh
3. Lo
4. Yea
5. O
6. Yea
7. Behold
8. Oh
9. Lo
10. Yea
11. Lo
12. Yea
13. Behold

FINAL TEST ON PARTS OF SPEECH

I.
1. noun
2. pronoun
3. verb
4. adverb
5. adjective
6. preposition
7. conjunction
8. interjection

II.
1. e
2. b
3. f
4. d
5. h
6. a
7. g
8. c

III.
1. a
2. an
3. the

IV.
1. PR
2. CM
3. CM
4. CM
5. PR
6. CM
7. PR
8. CM
9. PR

V.
1. nominative
2. possessive
3. objective

VI.
1. masculine
2. feminine
3. neuter

VII.
1. this
2. that
3. these
4. those

VIII. Answers will vary. See Lesson 4-C — all, another, any, both, each, either, every, few, many, most, much, neither, no, other, several, some

IX. Answers will vary. See Lesson 3-C — is, am, are, was, were, shall be, being, will be, have been, has been, had been, shall have been, will have been, seem, become, appear, remain, get, grow, stay, taste, feel, smell, sound.

X. 1. and
    2. but
    3. or
    4. nor
    5. for
    6. so
    7. yet

XI. 1. noun, preposition
     2. adverb, verb
     3. adjective, verb
     4. pronoun, noun
     5. verb, preposition
     6. adjective, adjective
     7. pronoun, adjective
     8. pronoun, adverb, noun
     9. interjection, pronoun
    10. verb, adjective

Chapter 9

EXERCISE 1
1. Jesus
2. James – John
3. men
4. fame
5. people
6. Jesus
7. multitude

EXERCISE 2
1. Jesus
2. James – John
3. Jesus
4. you
5. you

EXERCISE 3
1. people
2. example
3. river
4. peace
5. rod – branch

EXERCISE 4
1. Paul
2. Christians
3. Apphia – Archippus
4. letters
5. relationship
6. Onesimus – he
7. Paul
8. Onesimus, Philemon, Paul
9. God, God
10. Obedience, sympathy, brotherhood

EXERCISE 5

Answers will vary. See Lesson 3-C.

EXERCISE 6

2. it – power (P.N.)
3. Jesus Christ – same (P.N.)
4. Faith – substance (P.N.)

5. angels – spirits [P.N.]
   who – heirs [P.N.]
6. Jesus Christ – sin [P.N.]
7. to live – Christ [P.N.]
   to die – gain [P.N.]
8. This – day [P.N.]
9. Jesus Christ – vine [P.N.]
   we – branches [P.N.]
10. person – apple [P.N.]

EXERCISE 7

2. you, gods [D.O.]

3. you, image [D.O.]

4. you, yourself [D.O.], them [D.O.]

5. Lord, mercy [D.O.], him [D.O.], that, commandments [D.O.]

6. you, day [D.O.]

7. Everyone, father [D.O.] – mother [D.O.]

8. commandment, promise [D.O.]

9. we, we – adultery [D.O.]

   we, we – witness [D.O.]

10. Christian – house [D.O.], wife [D.O.], manservant [D.O.], maidservant [D.O.], thing [D.O.]

EXERCISE 8

1. Christ, multitudes, he, mouth [D.O.], people [D.O.] [D.O.]
2. poor, blessed [P.N.], theirs, kingdom [P.N.]

3. meek, blessed [P.N.], they, earth [D.O.]

4. merciful, blessed [P.N.], they, mercy [D.O.]
5. Christian, light [P.N.]

15

     D.O.   D.O.

6. <u>men</u>, candle, candle

     D.O.   D.O.

7. <u>they</u>, candle, <u>it</u>, light

        D.O.

8. <u>Christians</u>, light

      D.O.

9. <u>people</u>, work

      D.O.

10. <u>works</u>, Father

EXERCISE 9

       I.O. D.O.

2. <u>Everyone</u>, God, tithe

     I.O.   D.O.   D.O.

3. <u>God</u>, Bezaleel, wisdom, tabernacle

     I.O.   D.O.

4. <u>God</u>, Moses, dimensions

      I.O.   D.O.

5. <u>Israelites</u>, leaders, amount

       D.O.   D.O.

6. <u>children</u>, tabernacle, equipment

     I.O. D.O.

7. <u>writer</u>, us, story

       D.O.

8. <u>Lord</u>, commandments

     I.O. D.O.

9. <u>God</u>, Moses, tables

EXERCISE 10

Answers will vary. See Lesson 6-A.

EXERCISE 11

    O.P.   O.P.   O.P.

1. (for you), (of your member), (into hell)

    O.P.   O.P.

2. (for an eye), (for a tooth)

      O.P.   O.P.

3. (on the right cheek), (to him)

    O.P.

4. (to them)

     O.P.   O.P.

5. (of your Father), (in heaven)

6. (before men) — O.P.

7. (in secret) — O.P.

EXERCISE 12

1. Father, heaven
   O.P. over heaven

2. Hallowed, name
   P.N. over Hallowed

3. will, earth, it, heaven
   O.P. over earth, O.P. over heaven

4. He, us, bread
   I.O. over us, D.O. over bread

5. He, us, debts, we debtors
   I.O. over us, D.O. over debts, D.O. over debtors

6. He, us, temptation, us, evil
   D.O. over us, O.P. over temptation, D.O. over us, O.P. over evil

7. God, kingdom, power, glory
   O.P over kingdom

8. (you), hypocrite, you
   P.N. over you

9. Hypocrites, faces, men, what, they
   D.O. over men, D.O. over they

10. Christians, secret
    O.P. over secret

11. God, them
    D.O. over them

11. God, searcher, hearts
    P.V. over searcher, O.P. over hearts

EXERCISE 13

1. Eve's
2. God's
3. Noah's
4.
5. moment's
6.
7. father-in-law's
8.
9. fishermen's
10.

17

EXERCISE 14

2. . . . woman, <u>Adam and Eve</u>,
3. . . . Tempter, <u>Satan</u>, . . . (commas may be omitted here.)
4. . . . salvation, the <u>promise</u> of a coming Redeemer,
5. . . . Flood, a destructive <u>force</u>,
6. . . . mercy, the rainbow <u>covenant</u>.
7. . . . Babel, the <u>site</u> of a tall tower,
8. Abraham, a <u>friend</u> of God,
9. Abraham, the <u>Father</u> of the Faithful,
10. . . . Enoch, the <u>man</u>
11. . . . Genesis, <u>Jacob</u> and <u>Joseph</u>,

EXERCISE 15

2. Noah, the ark builder, was ridiculed by his contemporaries.
3. The Lord had no respect for Cain's offering, the fruit of the ground.
4. The Lord respected Abel's offering, the firstlings of his flock and the fat thereof.
5. Methuselah, Enoch's son, lived nine hundred sixty and nine years.
6. Everyone should memorize Genesis 3:15, the first Messianic Prophecy.
7. Genesis 9:6, a verse in the Bible, supplies the Christian with evidence that capital punishment should be allowed.
8. Jacob, a crafty young man, secured his birthright by duping Esau.
9. Later Jacob, a man of prayer, was transformed.
10. Joseph, Jacob's son, became a renowned ruler in Egypt.
11. Abraham, a man whose trust was in God, left his home in Ur to follow God.

EXERCISE 16

1. <u>Lord</u>, <u>Lord</u>,
2. <u>Jesus</u>,
3. <u>Sir</u>,
4. <u>Master</u>,
5. <u>Lord</u>,
6. fearful, <u>you</u>

EXERCISE 17

d. subject
e. direct object
f. direct object
g. object of preposition
h. subject
i. appositive
j. direct object

k. object of preposition
l. direct object
m. subject
n. direct object
o. possessive
p. subject
q. predicate nominative
r. direct object
s. noun of direct address
t. indirect object
u. direct object

EXERCISE 18

1. men ^{O.C.}

2. wise ^{O.C.}

3.

4. truths ^{R.O.}

5. whole ^{O.C.}

I. 1. subject
2. direct object
3. indirect object
4. object of a preposition
5. predicate nominative
6. appositive
7. noun of direct address
8. possessive

II. 1. object of preposition
2. direct object
3. subject
4. possessive
5. indirect object
6. noun of direct address
7. appositive
8. predicate nominative

III. 1. object of a preposition
2. subject, subject
3. object of a preposition
4. direct object
5. possessive
6. noun of direct address
7. predicate nominative, possessive
8. appositive

Chapter 10

NOTE: It is recommended that students review Chapter 2 thoroughly before taking Final Test on Pronouns.

EXERCISE 1

I	we
you	you
he, she, it	they

EXERCISE 2
1. we
2. he or she
3. I
4. she
5. they
6. we

EXERCISE 3

Answers will vary. See Chapter 3-C.

EXERCISE 4
1. he
2. he, I
3. they
4. we
5. she
6. he, he
7. he
8. they

EXERCISE 5

me	us
you	you
him, her, it	them

EXERCISE 6
1. me
2. us
3. us
4. us
5. us, us

EXERCISE 7
1. us
2. you, me
3. you

EXERCISE 8

1. us
2. me
3. me
4. you
5. him

EXERCISE 9

1. he
2. me
3. they
4. her
5. me
6. we
7. us
8. she
9. she
10. me, him

EXERCISE 10

1. me
2. they
3. us
4. they
5. I
6. we
7. us
8. ours
9. themselves
10. himself, I

EXERCISE 11

1. whosoever
2. who
3. whom
4. whom
5. whom

Test on Chapter 10

I. 1. nominative
    2. objective
    3. possessive

II. | | |
     |:---:|:---:|
     | I | we |
     | you | you |
     | he, she, it | they |

III. | | |
     |:---:|:---:|
     | me | us |
     | you | you |
     | him, her, it | them |

IV. | | |
     |:---:|:---:|
     | my, mine | our, ours |
     | your, yours | your, yours |
     | his, her, hers, its | their theirs |

V. 1. a. nominative
       b. objective
    2. c. nominative
       d. objective
    3. e. possessive
       f. objective
    4. g. nominative
       h. nominative
       i. possessive
    5. j. nominative

VI. 1. personal   I, you, etc
     2. demonstrative   this, that, these, those
     3. intensive   myself, yourself, etc.
     4. reflexive   myself, yourself, etc.
     5. interrogative   who, whose, whom, which, what
     6. indefinite   everyone, all, it, anybody, each, etc.
     7. relative   who, whose, whom, which, what

Students may select any 5 of the above.

VII. 1. interrogative
     2. personal
     3. indefinite
     4. personal
     5. demonstrative
     6. personal
     7. intensive/reflexive
     8. personal, relative, demonstrative, intensive/reflexive

23

VIII. 2. who   d. interrogative
       he   e. personal – predicate nominative
       that   f. relative pronoun
    3. I   g. personal – subject
       that   h. relative pronoun
       I   i. personal – subject
    4. I   j. personal – subject
       you   k. personal – object of preposition
       my   l. personal – possessive pronoun
       you   m. personal – direct object
    5. I   n. personal – subject
       myself   o. reflexive pronoun

Chapter 11

EXERCISE 1

1. irregular
2. irregular
3. regular
4. irregular
5. regular
6. irregular
7. regular
8. regular
9. regular
10. regular

EXERCISE 2

1. —, beginning, began, begun
2. behold, —, beheld, have beheld
3. burn, burning, —, have burned
4. forgive, forgiving, forgave, —
5. play, —, played, have played
6. —, kneeling, knelt, have knelt
7. cry, crying, cried, —
8. pass, passing, —, have passed
9. —, creating, created, have created
10. raise, —, raised, have raised

EXERCISE 3

I work	we work
you work	you work
he, she, it works	they work

EXERCISE 4

I eat	we eat
you eat	you eat
he, she, it eats	they eat

EXERCISE 5

I worked	we worked
you worked	you worked
he, she, it worked	they worked

EXERCISE 6

I went	we went
you went	you went
he, she, it went	they went

EXERCISE 7

1. fell
2. threw
3. knew
4. did
5. saw
6. brought

EXERCISE 8

1. followed
2. was
3. came
4. said

EXERCISE 9

I shall work	we shall work
you will work	you will work
he, she, it will work	they will work

EXERCISE 10

I shall eat	we shall eat
you will eat	you will eat
he, she, it will eat	they will eat

EXERCISE 11

1. will – promise
2. shall – promise
   shall – promise
3. shall – future
4. will – promise
5. shall – promise
   shall – promise
6. will – determination
   will – determination

EXERCISE 12

1. present
2. future
3. future
4. present
5. past

EXERCISE 13

1. believe
2. believed
3. will believe
4. hope
5. hoped
6. will hope

EXERCISE 14

I have worked	we have worked
you have worked	you have worked
he, she, it has worked	they have worked

EXERCISE 15

I have eaten	we have eaten
you have eaten	you have eaten
he, she, it has eaten	they have eaten

EXERCISE 16

I had worked	we had worked
you had worked	you had worked
he, she, it had worked	they had worked

EXERCISE 17

I had eaten	we had eaten
you had eaten	you had eaten
he, she, it had eaten	they had eaten

EXERCISE 18

I shall have worked	we shall have worked
you will have worked	you will have worked
he, she it will have worked	they will have worked

EXERCISE 19

I shall have eaten	we shall have eaten
you will have eaten	you will have eaten
he, she, it will have eaten	they will have eaten

EXERCISE 20

1. present	6. past
2. past	7. future
3. future perfect	8. past perfect
4. past	9. past
5. present perfect	10. past perfect

EXERCISE 21

PRESENT

i love	we love
you love	you love
he, she, it loves	they love

PAST

I loved	we loved
you loved	you loved
he, she, it loved	they loved

FUTURE

I shall love	we shall love
you will love	you will love
he, she, it will love	they will love

PRESENT PERFECT

I have loved	we have loved
you have loved	you have loved
he, she, it has loved	they have loved

PAST PERFECT

I had loved	we had loved
you had loved	you had loved
he, she, it had loved	they had loved

FUTURE PERFECT

I shall have loved	we shall have loved
you will have loved	you will have loved
he, she, it will have loved	they will have loved

EXERCISE 22

1. active, passive
2. active, passive
3. active, active
4. active
5. passive
6. active, active, active

EXERCISE 23

PRESENT

I am loved	we are loved
you are loved	you are loved
he, she, it is loved	they are loved

PAST

I was loved	we were loved
you were loved	you were loved
he, she, it was loved	they were loved

FUTURE

I shall be loved	we shall be loved
you will be loved	you will be loved
he, she, it will be loved	they will be loved

PRESENT PERFECT

I have been loved	we have been loved
you have been loved	you have been loved
he, she, it has been loved	they have been loved

PAST PERFECT

I had been loved	we had been loved
you had been loved	you had been loved
he, she, it had been loved	they had been loved

FUTURE PERFECT

I shall have been loved	we shall have been loved
you will have been loved	you will have been loved
he, she, it will have been loved	they will have been loved

EXERCISE 24

1. be
2. were
3. be
4. forbid
5. were

Test on Chapter 11

I. 1. present
    2. present participle
    3. past
    4. past participle

II. d or ed

III. irregular verbs

IV. 1. doing, did, have done, or has done
    2. reading, read, have read, or has read

V.

Present

I am	we are
you are	you are
he, she, it is	they are

Past

I was	we were
you were	you were
he, she, it was	they were

Future

I shall be	we shall be
you will be	you will be
he, she, it will be	they will be

Present Perfect

I have been	we have been
you have been	you have been
he, she it has been	they have been

Past Perfect

I had been	we had been
you had been	you had been
he, she, it had been	they had been

Future Perfect

I shall have been	we shall have been
you will have been	you will have been
he, she, it will have been	they will have been

VI. 1. active
     2. passive
     3. I am bringing
     4. they did bring
     5. we shall be brought

VII. indicative, imperative, subjunctive

Chapter 12

EXERCISE 1
Answers will vary. See Lesson 3-C.

EXERCISE 2
1. wiser
2. stronger
3. precious
4. gentle
5. dear

EXERCISE 3
1. predicate adjective
2. predicate noun, predicate noun
3. predicate adjective
4. predicate adjective
5. predicate adjective
6. predicate adjective
7. none
8. predicate noun
9. predicate pronoun

EXERCISE 4
1. positive
2. comparative
3. superlative

EXERCISE 5
1. comparative
2. positive
3. superlative

EXERCISE 6
1. most difficult of all the stories
2. unique
3. highest
4. more
5. most
6. quickest
7. quicker

Chapter 13

EXERCISE 1

1. heavier
2. anyone else
3. bad
4. delicious
5. almost
6. surely
7. well
8. really
9. well
10. Surely

Test on Adjectives and Adverbs

I. nouns and pronouns

II. verbs, adverbs, adjectives

III. positive, comparative, superlative

IV. comparative

V. superlative

VI.
1. better   best
2. taller   tallest
3. easier   easiest
4. better   best
5. more recent   most recent

VII.
1. really
2. almost
3. surely
4. smarter
5. most clever of all
6. prettier than anyone else in the realm
7. almost always
8. bad
9. dreadful
10. surely

Chapter 14

EXERCISE 1

1. promises
2. house
3. building
4. Spirit
5. ministers

EXERCISE 2

1. believeth
2. is made
3. shall call
4. shall call
5. shall believe
6. shall hear

EXERCISE 3

1. a. adverb
   b. adjective
   c. adverb
2. d. adverb
   e. adverb
   f. adjective
   g. adjective

Test on Chapter 14

I.   1. could have been
     2. besides
     3. Paul
     4. Between you and me, would have been
     5. Between Paul and Timothy

II. 1. a. by faith–adverb
        b. with God–adverb or adjective
        c. through our Lord Jesus Christ–adverb
     2. d. By whom–adverb
        e. by faith–adverb
        f. into this grace–adverb
        g. in hope–adverb
        h. of the glory–adjective
        i. of God–adjective
     3. j. toward us–adverb
        k. in that–adverb
        l. for us–adverb

Note: 1. The phrase "with God" may be considered an adjective phrase because it stands next to a noun. It may be considered an adverbial phrase if students feel it answers the question: How?
2. In v. 8, the phrase "in that" may be confusing to students and the teacher may need to explain its usage.

I. 1. and
    2. but
    3. or
    4. nor
    5. so
    6. yet

Any 5 are acceptable.

II. 1. neither . . . nor
    2. both . . . and
    3. not . . . but
    4. not only . . . but also

Any 3 are acceptable.

III. 1. different from
     2. like
     3. in which
     4. On account of
     5. etc.

Test on Part 2

I. 1. b. object of a preposition
      c. possessive
      d. subject
      e. direct object
   2. f. indirect object
      g. subject
   3. h. predicate noun
      i. predicate noun
      j. appositive
   4. k. noun of direct address
      l. objective complement

II. 1. a. object of preposition
       b. indirect object
       c. possessive
    2. d. direct object
       e. subject
       f. direct object
    3. g. predicate pronoun

III. 1. set
     2. known
     3. were
     4. gone
     5. trust, will
     6. brought, fallen, risen

IV. 1. a. active
       b. active
    2. c. passive
    3. d. passive

V. 1. weary
   2. mindful, man
   3. angry
   4. perfect, sure
   5. right, pure

VI. 1. — , lovelier, loveliest
    2. little, — , least
    3. much, more, —
    4. — , circular, circular

Chapter 16

EXERCISE 1

1. infinitive
2. participial or participle
3. gerund

EXERCISE 2

1. *smitten, afflicted, him*
2. *oppressed, afflicted, he*
3. *wanting, you*
4. *trusting, heart*
5. *converting, law*
   making, testimony

EXERCISE 3

1. *(enlightening the eyes), commandment*
2. *(with the saving strength of his right hand) strength*
3. *(waxing confident by my bonds), many*
4. *(supposing to add affliction to my bonds), one*
5. *(knowing that I am set for the defense of the Gospel), other*
6. *(having a desire to depart and to be with Christ), I*
7. *(having this confidence), I*
8. *(not regarding his life), he*
9. *(being fruitful in every good work), ye*
   (increasing in the knowledge of God), ye
10. *(Strengthened with all might), ye*
11. *(Giving thanks unto the Father), ye*

Chapter 17

EXERCISE 1

1. (with rejoicing and singing) – object of preposition
2. (In praising and thanking the Lord) –object of preposition
3. (since my coming) – object of preposition
4. (of the crying) – object of preposition
5. (the shouting) –direct object
6. (giving him drink) –direct object
   (drinking) – direct object

EXERCISE 2

1. gerund
2. gerund
3. verb
4. participle
5. participle, participle
6. gerund, gerund
7. verb

Chapter 18

EXERCISE 1

1. (to fulfill the Word of God)
2. (to abide still at Ephesus)
3. (to save sinners)
4. (not to blaspheme)
5. (to be saved), (to come into the knowledge of the truth)
6. (to be testified in due time)
7. (to teach), (to usurp authority over the man), (to be in silence)

EXERCISE 2

1. (you to rise up early, to sit up late, to eat the bread of sorrows.)
2. (brethren to dwell together in unity)
3. NONE
4. (them have dominion over the fish of the sea)
   [*To* is understood.]

● See note on pg. 142.

5. (heart ... soul to seek the Lord your God.)

Test on Verbals

I. 1. infinitive
   2. gerund
   3. participle

II. 1. verb, to, noun, adjective, adverb
    2. verb, adjective
    3. verb, -ing, noun

III. a. (to please him) – infinitive
     b. (being warned of God of things not seen as yet) – participle
     c. (moved with fear) – participle
     d. (to the saving of his house) – gerund
     e. (not having received the promises) – participle
     f. (having seen them afar off) – participle
     g. (to be called the son of Pharaoh's daughter) – infinitive
     h. (choosing rather) – participle
     i. (to suffer affliction with the people of God) – infinitive
     j. (to enjoy the pleasures of sin for a season) – infinitive
     k. (chastening for the present) – gerund
     l. (to be joyous) – infinitive

Chapter 19

EXERCISE 1

    1. declarative .
    2. interrogative ?
    3. declarative .
    4. elliptical ! or ?
    5. interrogative ?
    6. imperative .
    7. declarative .
    8. declarative .
    9. interrogative ?
   10. exclamatory !

EXERCISE 2

    1. declarative
    2. interrogative
    3. imperative
    4. exclamatory
    5. elliptical

EXERCISE 1

1. labor; compound
2. works; houses; compound
3. no punctuation – simple
4. no punctuation – simple
5. head; however, compound
6. sorrows, compound
7. no punctuation – simple
8. no punctuation – simple
9. no punctuation – simple
10. season, compound

EXERCISE 1

    1. adverbial clause

    2. prepositional phrase

    3. adverb

    4. adverbial clause

    5. adverbial clause

EXERCISE 2

    Answers will vary. See Lesson 21-D.

EXERCISE 3

    1. (When the first . . . arrived,)

    2. (as Jesus . . . them.)

    3. none

    4. (Now when the even was come,)

    5. (As they did eat,)

    6. (when he would break . . . kingdom.)

    7. (When they had . . . hymn.)

EXERCISE 4

    1. who   4. which

    2. whose   5. that

    3. whom   6. what

EXERCISE 5

    1. (whom Jesus took with him to Gethsemane)

    2. (who wanted . . . will,)

    3. (which was very bitter,)

    4. none

    5. (who was . . . twelve,)

    6. (that betrayed Jesus)

    7. (which were with Jesus)

    8. (that take the sword)

EXERCISE 6

    1. (that after . . . passover!) – direct object

    2. (that Jesus . . . Father?) – direct object

    3. (that Jesus . . . blasphemy) – direct object

    4. (That Jesus . . . blasphemy) – subject

    5. (that Jesus . . . God.) – subject complement

EXERCISE 7

1. (when . . . come.) – adverb clause
2. (when. . . him) – adverb clause
3. (which had betrayed him) –adjective clause
   (when he saw that he was condemned) – adverb clause
   (that he was condemned) – noun clause
4. (that I . . . blood.) – noun clause
5. (When he . . . elders,) – adverb clause
6. (whom they would) – adjective clause
7. (that for envy . . . him) – noun clause
8. (when he . . . seat,) – adverb clause

Final Test on Part IV

1. complex – adjective clause
2. simple
3. complex – noun
4. complex, compound – adverb, noun, noun
5. simple
6. simple
7. simple
8. complex, compound – adverb
9. compound
10. compound

FINAL TEST

1. 16
2. 12
2. 1
4. 11
5. 15
6. 22
7. 5
8. 8
9. 20
10. 3 or 6
11. 14
12. 7
13. 19
14. 6
15. 9
16. 13
17. 10
18. 2
19. 25
20. 21
21. 17
22. 4
23. 26
24. 23
25. 24
26. 18